Hymns for children, and persons of riper years. The fourth edition.

Charles Wesley

ECCO
PRINT EDITIONS

Eighteenth Century
Collections Online
Print Editions

Gale ECCO Print Editions

Relive history with *Eighteenth Century Collections Online*, now available in print for the independent historian and collector. This series includes the most significant English-language and foreign-language works printed in Great Britain during the eighteenth century, and is organized in seven different subject areas including literature and language; medicine, science, and technology; and religion and philosophy. The collection also includes thousands of important works from the Americas.

The eighteenth century has been called "The Age of Enlightenment." It was a period of rapid advance in print culture and publishing, in world exploration, and in the rapid growth of science and technology – all of which had a profound impact on the political and cultural landscape. At the end of the century the American Revolution, French Revolution and Industrial Revolution, perhaps three of the most significant events in modern history, set in motion developments that eventually dominated world political, economic, and social life.

In a groundbreaking effort, Gale initiated a revolution of its own: digitization of epic proportions to preserve these invaluable works in the largest online archive of its kind. Contributions from major world libraries constitute over 175,000 original printed works. Scanned images of the actual pages, rather than transcriptions, recreate the works *as they first appeared.*

Now for the first time, these high-quality digital scans of original works are available via print-on-demand, making them readily accessible to libraries, students, independent scholars, and readers of all ages.

For our initial release we have created seven robust collections to form one the world's most comprehensive catalogs of 18th century works.

Initial Gale ECCO Print Editions collections include:

History and Geography
Rich in titles on English life and social history, this collection spans the world as it was known to eighteenth-century historians and explorers. Titles include a wealth of travel accounts and diaries, histories of nations from throughout the world, and maps and charts of a world that was still being discovered. Students of the War of American Independence will find fascinating accounts from the British side of conflict.

Social Science
Delve into what it was like to live during the eighteenth century by reading the first-hand accounts of everyday people, including city dwellers and farmers, businessmen and bankers, artisans and merchants, artists and their patrons, politicians and their constituents. Original texts make the American, French, and Industrial revolutions vividly contemporary.

Medicine, Science and Technology
Medical theory and practice of the 1700s developed rapidly, as is evidenced by the extensive collection, which includes descriptions of diseases, their conditions, and treatments. Books on science and technology, agriculture, military technology, natural philosophy, even cookbooks, are all contained here.

Literature and Language
Western literary study flows out of eighteenth-century works by Alexander Pope, Daniel Defoe, Henry Fielding, Frances Burney, Denis Diderot, Johann Gottfried Herder, Johann Wolfgang von Goethe, and others. Experience the birth of the modern novel, or compare the development of language using dictionaries and grammar discourses.

Religion and Philosophy
The Age of Enlightenment profoundly enriched religious and philosophical understanding and continues to influence present-day thinking. Works collected here include masterpieces by David Hume, Immanuel Kant, and Jean-Jacques Rousseau, as well as religious sermons and moral debates on the issues of the day, such as the slave trade. The Age of Reason saw conflict between Protestantism and Catholicism transformed into one between faith and logic -- a debate that continues in the twenty-first century.

Law and Reference
This collection reveals the history of English common law and Empire law in a vastly changing world of British expansion. Dominating the legal field is the *Commentaries of the Law of England* by Sir William Blackstone, which first appeared in 1765. Reference works such as almanacs and catalogues continue to educate us by revealing the day-to-day workings of society.

Fine Arts
The eighteenth-century fascination with Greek and Roman antiquity followed the systematic excavation of the ruins at Pompeii and Herculaneum in southern Italy; and after 1750 a neoclassical style dominated all artistic fields. The titles here trace developments in mostly English-language works on painting, sculpture, architecture, music, theater, and other disciplines. Instructional works on musical instruments, catalogs of art objects, comic operas, and more are also included.

The BiblioLife Network

This project was made possible in part by the BiblioLife Network (BLN), a project aimed at addressing some of the huge challenges facing book preservationists around the world. The BLN includes libraries, library networks, archives, subject matter experts, online communities and library service providers. We believe every book ever published should be available as a high-quality print reproduction; printed on-demand anywhere in the world. This insures the ongoing accessibility of the content and helps generate sustainable revenue for the libraries and organizations that work to preserve these important materials.

The following book is in the "public domain" and represents an authentic reproduction of the text as printed by the original publisher. While we have attempted to accurately maintain the integrity of the original work, there are sometimes problems with the original work or the micro-film from which the books were digitized. This can result in minor errors in reproduction. Possible imperfections include missing and blurred pages, poor pictures, markings and other reproduction issues beyond our control. Because this work is culturally important, we have made it available as part of our commitment to protecting, preserving, and promoting the world's literature.

GUIDE TO FOLD-OUTS MAPS and OVERSIZED IMAGES

The book you are reading was digitized from microfilm captured over the past thirty to forty years. Years after the creation of the original microfilm, the book was converted to digital files and made available in an online database.

In an online database, page images do not need to conform to the size restrictions found in a printed book. When converting these images back into a printed bound book, the page sizes are standardized in ways that maintain the detail of the original. For large images, such as fold-out maps, the original page image is split into two or more pages

Guidelines used to determine how to split the page image follows:

• Some images are split vertically; large images require vertical and horizontal splits.
• For horizontal splits, the content is split left to right.
• For vertical splits, the content is split from top to bottom.
• For both vertical and horizontal splits, the image is processed from top left to bottom right.

HYMNS

FOR

CHILDREN,

AND PERSONS

Of RIPER YEARS.

THE FOURTH EDITION.

LONDON·

Printed by J. PARAMORE, at the Foundry, Moorfields·
And fold at the New Chapel, City-Road, and at the Rev Mr.
Wesley's Preaching Houfes in Town and Country. 1784.

✤ ✤ ✤ ✤ ✤ ✤ ✤ ✤ ✤ ✤

H Y M N S

F O R

C H I L D R E N, &c.

H Y M N I.

Of G O D.

1 HAIL Father, Son, and Holy Ghoſt,
    One God in Perſons Three,
Of Thee we make our early boaſt,
    Our ſongs we make of Thee.

2 Thou neither canſt be felt, or ſeen,
    Thou art a Spirit pure,
Who from eternity haſt been, -
    And always ſhalt endure.

3 Preſent alike in every place,
    Thy Godhead we adore,
Beyond the bounds of time and ſpace
    Thou dwelléſt for evermore.

4 In wiſdom infinite Thou art,
    Thine eye doth all things ſee,
And every thought of every heart
    Is fully known to Thee.

5 Whate'er Thou wilt, in earth below
   Thou doft, in heav'n above ·
   But chiefly we rejoice to know
   The Almighty God is Love.

6 Thou lovéft whate'er thy hands have made;
   Thy goodnefs we rehearfe,
   In fhining characters difplayéd
   Throughout the univerfe.

7 Mercy, and love, and endlefs grace
   O'er all thy works do reign:
   But moftly thou delightéft to blefs
   Thy fav'rite creature, Man.

8 Wherefore let evéry creature give
   To Thee the praife defignéd;
   But chiefly, Lord, the thanks receive,
   The hearts of all mankind.

HYMN II.

Of the Creation and Fall of Man.

1   O All-creating God,
        At whofe fupreme decree
   Our body rofe a breathing clod,
        Our fouls fprang forth from Thee,
        For this Thou haft defignéd,
        And forméd us man for this,
   To know, and love Thyfelf, and find
        In Thee our endlefs blifs.

2   Thou the firft happy pair
        In paradife didft place,
   To reap the joys and pleafures there,
        And fing the Giver's praife.

Of

Of all the trees, but one
Forbidden was, to prove
Their due regard to God alone,
Their firm obedient love.

3 But O they rafhly took
Of the forbidden tree,
Thine eafy, fole commandment broke,
And finnéd, and fell from Thee.
Of their wide-fpreading fault
The fad effects we find,
Anguifh, and fin, and death it brought
On us, and all mankind.

4 Infected by their ftain
In fin we all are born,
And liable to grief and pain,
Till we to duft return.
To evéry fin inclinéd,
Selfifh we are, and proud,
Our will perverfe, our carnal mind
Is enmity to God.

5 Dead to the things above,
While in our loft eftate,
Children of wrath, the world we love;
And Thee by nature hate,
In pining griefs and cares
We fpend our wretched breath,
And die the miferable heirs
Of everlafting death.

H Y M N III.

Of the Redemption of Man.

1 SAVIOUR from fin, from death, from hell,
Thee, Jefus Chrift, with joy we own,
The man who lovéd our fouls fo well,
The Father's everlafting Son.

2 Thou for our fake a Man waft made,
    The burthen of a virgin's womb,
Didft live and fuffer in our ftead,
    And life triumphant from the tomb.

3 What hath thy death for finners gained?
    What hath thy life to finners givén?
For evéry foul of man obtainéd
    Pardon, and holinefs and heavén.

4 Soon as our broken hearts repent,
    Soon as I do in Thee believe,
The power into my foul is fent,
    And then my pardon I receive.

H Y M N IV.

The fame.

1 O Could I now to God return,
    With all fincerity of grief,
My finfulnefs, and folly mourn,
    My guilt and helplefs unbelief!

2 O could I now the faith obtain,
    That evidence of things unfeen,
And know the Lamb, for finners flain,
    For me, the finfulleft of men!

3 Come, Holy Ghoft, the grace impart,
    Reveal the dying Deity,
And feelingly convince my heart
    He lov'd, and gave himfelf for me.

4 The pardon on my confcience feal,
    Infpire the fenfe of fin forgivén,
And all my new-born foul fhall feel
    That holinefs is prefent heavén.

HYMN

H Y M N V.

The fame.

1 HAPPY the man who Jefus knows,
    By holy faith to Jefus joinéd!
His pure believing heart o'erflows
    With love to God and all mankind.

2 Redeeméd from all iniquity,
    From evéry evil work and word,
From evéry finful temper free,
    He lives devoted to his Lord.

3 Little and vile in his own eyes,
    All good he gives to God alone :
Savéd from felf-will he ever cries
    Lord, not my will, but thine be done !

4 Savéd from the love of all below,
    Heavénward his evéry wifh afpires ;
Nothing but Chrift refolvéd to know,
    God, only God, his heart defires.

5 Savéd from all evil words, he fpeaks
    For God, and minifters his grace,
Savéd from all evil deeds he feeks
    In all to' advance his Maker's praife.

6 Whether he eats, in faith, or drinks,
    He fpreads his Maker's praife abroad,
Whether he acts, or fpeaks, or thinks,
    He only aims to' exalt his God.

H Y M N VI.

Of the Means of Grace.

1 GOD of all-alluring grace,
   Thee through Jesus Christ we praise,
   Father, in thy Spirit's power,
   Thee we for thy grace adore.

2 Sent in Jesu's mighty name,
   Grace with God from heaven came,
   Grace on all mankind bestowed,
   Grace, the life and power of God.

3 Us, whoe'er the gift receive,
   It enables to believe,
   Helps our soul's infirmity
   Still to live and die with Thee.

4 In the means thou hast enjoined,
   All who seek the grace shall find,
   In the prayer, the fast, the word,
   In the supper of their Lord.

5 Thus the saints of ancient days
   Waited, and obtained thy grace,
   Drank the blood by Jesus shed,
   Daily on his body fed.

6 Thus the whole assembly joined
   Jesus in the midst to find,
   Prayer presenting to the skies,
   Morn and evening sacrifice.

7 Jointly praying, and apart,
   Each to Thee poured out his heart,
   Solemnly thy grace implored,
   Still continued in the word.

8 Search'd the fcripture day and night,
    (All their comfort and delight
    There to catch thy Spirit's power)
    Heard, and read, and liv'd them o'er.

9 Twice a week they fafted then,
    Pureft of the fons of men,
    Choiceft veffels of thy grace,
    Patterns to the faithful race.

10 Still to us they fpeak, though dead,
    Bid us in their footfteps tread,
    Bid us never dare remove
    From the channels of thy love.

11 Never will we hence depart,
    Till our all in all Thou art,
    Till from outward means we fly,
    Till we on thy bofom die.

H Y M N VII.

Of Hell.

1 WRETCHED fouls, who live in fin,
        Who their Lord by deeds deny!
    Tophet yawns to take them in,
        Soon as their frail bodies die,
    They their due reward fhall feel,
    Dreadfully thruft down to hell.

2 Dark and bottomlefs the pit
        Which on them its mouth fhall clofe:
    Never fhall they 'fcape from it
        There they fhall in endlefs woes
    Weep, and wail, and gnafh their teeth,
    Die an everlafting death.

3 There

3 There their tortur'd bodies lie,
   Scorchéd by the confuming fire,
There their fouls in torments cry,
   Rackéd with pride and fierce defire :
Fear, and grief their fpirits tear,
Rage, and envy, and defpair.

4 Evéry part its curfe fuftains,
   Every faculty of foul,
All the powér of hellifh pains
   Joins to make their meafure full,
Fiends, themfelves, and confcience join,
Heightenéd all by wrath divine.

5 There they lie, alas, how long !
   Never can they hope releafe,
Not a drop to cool their tongue,
   Not an hour, a moment's eafe :
Damnéd they are, and ftill fhall be,
Damnéd to all eternity !

H Y M N VIII.

Of Heaven.

1 WHERE fhall true believers go,
   When from the flefh they fly ?
Glorious joys ordained to know,
   They mount above the fky,
To that bright celeftial place,
   There they fhall in raptures live,
More than tongue can e'er exprefs,
   Or heart can e'er conceive.

2 When they once are enteréd there,
   Their mourning days are o'er,
Pain, and fin, and want, and care,
   And fighing are no more .

Subject

Subject then to no decay,
   Heavenly bodies they put on,
Swifter than the lightning's ray,
   And brighter than the sun.

3 But their greatest happiness,
   Their highest joy shall be,
God their Saviour to possess,
   To know, and love, and see :
With that beatific sight
   Glorious extasy is given,
This is the supreme delight,
   And makes a heaven of heaven.

4 Him beholding face to face,
   To Him they glory give,
Bless his name, and sing his praise,
   As long as God shall live.
While eternal ages roll,
   Thus employed in heaven they are :
Lord, receive my happy soul,
   With all thy servants there !

H Y M N IX.

1 TEACHER, Guide of young beginners,
   Let a child approach to Thee,
Thee, who camest to ransom sinners,
   Thee who diedst to ransom me .
Into thy protection take me,
   Full of goodness as thou art,
After thine own image make me,
   Make me after thy own heart.

2 Exercise the potter's power,
   Over this unshapen clay :
Call me in the morning-hour,
   Teach my simpleness the way :

With

With a tender awe infpire,
    That I never more may rove,
The faint fpark of good defire
    Blow into a flame of love.

3 O my everlafting Lover,
    Thee that I may love again,
To mine inmoft foul difcover
    All thy dying love for man,
By thy Spirit s infpiration
    Make thy depths of mercy known,
Seal the heir of true falvation,
    Then tranflate me to thy throne.

H Y M N X.

1 ALMIGHTY God, to Thee I cry,
    Affift a child's infirmity,
Nor let me with my lips draw nigh,
    While my heart wanders far from Thee,

2 Ah, never let me fpeak a word,
    But what with all my foul I mean;
Or lie to Thee, Thou glorious Lord,
    By whom my every thought is feen.

3 With what fubmiffive lowlinefs
    Shall I approach thy gracious throne ?
How can I hope by words to pleafe,
    To pleafe a God I have not known ?

4 I know not what to do, or fay,
    Till I thy bleffed Spirit receive,
And Jefus teaches me to pray,
    And Jefus teaches me to live.

HYMN

H Y M N XI.

1 GLORIOUS God, accept a heart
    That pants to fing thy praife:
Thou without beginning art,
    And without end of days·
Thou a Spirit invifible,
    Doft to none thy fulnefs fhew,
None thy Majefty can tell,
    Or all thy Godhead know.

2 All thine attributes we own,
    Thy wifdom, power, and might:
Happy in thyfelf alone,
    In goodnefs infinite,
Thou thy goodnefs haft difplayed,
    On thine every work impreft,
Lovéft whate'er thy hands have made.
    But man thou lovéft the beft,

3 Willing Thou, that all fhould know
    Thy faving truth, and live,
Doft to each or blifs or woe
    With ftrifteft juftice give:
Thou with perfeft rightéoufnefs
    Renderéft every man his due,
Faithful in thy promifes,
    And in thy threaténings too.

4 Thou art merciful to all
    Who truly turn to thee,
Hear me then for pardon call,
    And fhew thy grace to me ;
Me by mercy reconciléd,
    Me for Jefu's fake forgivén,
Me, receive, thy fav'rite child,
    To fing thy praife in heavén.

HYMN

HYMN XII.

1 O Thou whom none hath feen or known,
　But He that in thy bofom lies,
Thine heavenly beft-beloved Son,
　Creator both of earth and fkies,
He only knows and can explain
Thy Godhead to the fons of men.

2 Not all the things we read or hear
　Can Thee unto our fouls reveal,
Not all the art of man declare,
　Thy Spirit muft the fecret tell,
Into our deepeft darknefs fhine,
And manifeft the things divine.

3 Father of everlafting grace,
　The Spirit of the Son impart,
To us who humbly feek thy face,
　Who pray for light with all our heart,
And long to know thy bleffed will,
And all thy counfel to fulfil.

HYMN XIII.

1 THOU, O God, art good alone,
　(Praife to Thee alone be given)
Truly iffues from thy throne
　All the good in earth and heaven;
Good if e'er in man we fee,
Lord, it all proceeds from Thee.

2 Unaffifted by thy grace
　We can only evil do,
Wretched is the human race,
　Wretched more than words can fhow,
Till thy bleffing from above
Tells our hearts that God is love.

H Y M N XIV.

1 ALL powér to fave, O Lord, is thine,
    Receive this ruined foul of mine,
      Upon thy mercy caft,
Do with me what, and as Thou wilt,
But throughly purge away my guilt,
      And fave my foul at laft.

2 What I into thy hands commend,
    Keep, and continue to defend,
      In humble faith I pray,
Evil and danger turn afide,
And me, and my companions hide,
      Againft that awful day.

3 Then, Lord, by thine almighty powér
  Our bodies and our fouls reftore,
      Committed to thy care,
Our hidden life with Chrift reveal,
And lift us to thy heavénly hill,
      To fee thy glory there.

H Y M N XV.

1 MAKER, Saviour of mankind,
    Who haft on me beftowéd
An immortal foul, defignéd
    To be the houfe of God.
Come, and now refide in me,
    Never never to remove,
Make me juft, and good like Thee,
    And full of powér and love.

2 Bid me in thine image rife
    A faint, a creature new,
True, and merciful, and wife,
    And pure, and happy too.

B 2

This

'This thy primitive defign,
 That I fhould in Thee be bleft,
Should within the arms divine
 For ever, ever reft.

3 Let thy will on me be done,
 Fulfil my heart's defire,
Thee, to know, and love alone,
 And rife in rapture higher,
Thee defcending on a cloud
 When with ravifhéd eyes I fee,
Then I fhall be filléd with God
 To all eternity.

H Y M N XVI.

1 AUTHOR, and End of my defires,
 From whom my évery bleffing flowéd,
I *would* whate'er thy will requires,
 Whate'er thy will requires is good.

2 I would (but Thou muft give the powér)
 From all befide my will avert,
Nor ever grieve thy goodnefs more,
 Nor ever follow my own heart.

3 Spring of all good thy will I own,
 The fountain of all evil mine;
Father, let mine no more be done,
 Let all obey the will divine.

4 We came into the world to do
 The will of Him that placéd us here,
And who their own defires purfue,
 Can never in thy fight appear.

5 What then fhall of our fouls become
 Uféd our own pleafure to fulfil?
Eternal death muft be the doom
 Of all that follow their own will.

6 But O, to Thee for help we cry,
　　Save, or we fink into the pit,
　Ourfelves affift us to deny,
　　And to thy bleffed will fubmit.

7 Father, for Jefu's fake alone,
　　Thine all-fufficient grace impart,
　Save us, in honour of thy Son,
　　And God-ward turn the felfifh heart.

8 So fhall we evéry moment feel,
　　(When Thou the Holy Ghoft haft givén)
　To do our curled will, is hell,
　　To do thy bleffed will, is heavén.

H Y M N   XVII.

1 GOD is goodnefs, wifdom, powér,
　　Love Him, praife Him evermore,
　Let us ftrive and never ceafe,
　Him in evéry thing to pleafe.

2 Born for this intent we are,
　　Our Creator to declare,
　God to love, and ferve, and praife,
　God to honour all our days.

3 Lift we then our hearts to God,
　　Like the church above employéd,
　Day and night the angels fing
　Praifes to their heavénly king.

4 Him that fitteth on the throne,
　　Him that diéd for man to' atone,
　God, and the triumphant Lamb,
　They eternally proclaim.

5 Let us then to God afpire,
　　Rivals of the heavénly quire;
　Cherubim our faces wear,
　Let us their enjoyments fhare.

　　　　6 Holy,

6 Holy, holy, holy Lord,
   Live by heaven and earth adoréd,
   Filléd with Thee let all things cry,
   Glory be to God moſt high!

H Y M N   XVIII.

1 HAPPY man whom God doth aid!
   God our ſoul and body made,
   God on us in gracious ſhowérs
   Bleſſings evéry moment pours,
   Compaſſes with angel-bands,
   Bids them bear us in their hands:
   Parents, friends, 'twas God beſtowéd,
   Life, and all deſcends from God.

2 He this flowéry carpet ſpread,
   Made the earth on which we tread,
   God refreſhes in the air,
   Covers with the clothes we wear,
   Feeds us in the food we eat,
   Cheers us by the light and heat,
   Makes the ſun on us to ſhine;
   All our bleſſings are divine.

3 Give him then, and always give,
   Thanks for all that we receive.
   Man we for his kindneſs love,
   How much more our God above?
   Worthy, Thou, our heavénly Lord,
   To be honouréd and adoréd,
   God of all-creating grace,
   Take the everlaſting praiſe.

H Y M N   XIX.

1 BUT what are all the bleſſings, Lord,
   Which our frail bodies prove,
   Unleſs Thou to our ſouls afford
     The happineſs of love?

2 Our fouls (we above all defire)
   Our fouls vouchfafe to blefs,
And into our young hearts infpire
   The knowledge of thy grace.

3 We lack the wifdom from on high,
   For love on Thee we call,
Who never canft thyfelf deny
   But givéft thyfelf to all.

4 Then let us with thy gifts receive,
   The Giver from above,
And never fin, and never grieve,
   The God whom once we love.

H Y M N XX.

1 FATHER, to Thee thine own we give,
   Thy wifdom, powér, and goodnefs praife,
Thy benefits with thanks receive,
   And humbly fue for pard'ning grace,
Thy mercy and thy ftrength implore,
To keep us that we fin no more.

2 We pray, but with our lips alone,
   Till thou infufe the pure defire,
Till Thou to flefh convert the ftone,
   The gracious principle infpire,
The Supplicating Spirit impart,
And blefs us with a praying heart.

H Y M N XXI.

1 WHAT matters it to pray
   To God in Jefu's name,
Unlefs we feel the words we fay,
   And hang upon the Lamb?
The Lamb for finners flain,
   If ftrangers to his blood,
We only take his name in vain,
   And mock thé Almighty God.

2   Father of mercies, fhow
       What we by nature were,
Children of wrath, and doom'd below
       Eternal pains to bear,
       When Jefus Chrift thy Son
       For helplefs finners di'd,
That all who truft in him alone,
       May know Thee pacifi'd.

3   In Him if we believe,
       Thy mercies we partake,
Who all good things art pleaf'd to give
       To man for Jefu's fake.
       We durft not afk thine aid,
       Or hope to' obtain thy love,
But that his blood for us was fhed,
       And fpeaks for us above

4   Wherefore to Thee we cry,
       Through thy beloved Son,
And fix on Him our ftedfaft eye,
       Who ftands before thy throne;
       The good defires we feel,
       From Him, we own, they came,
And them, according to thy will,
       Prefent in Jefu's name.

5   Our prayers to his unite,
       And as thy Son's receive,
And give, who afk in Jefu's right,
       To us thy bleffing give,
       Whate er we thus defire,
       The fuit of Jefus is.
Hear then, and raife thy glory higher,
       By our eternal blifs.

H Y M N   XXII.

1 THOU, my God, art good and wife,
       And infinite in power,
Thee let all in earth and fkies
       Eternally adore:

                                Give

Give me thy converting grace,
  That I may obedient prove,
Serve my Maker all my days,
  And my Redeemer love.

2 For my life, and clothes, and food,
  And every comfort here,
Thee, my moſt indulgent God,
  I thank with heart ſincere ,
For the bleſſings numberleſs,
  Which thou haſt already givén,
For my ſmalleſt ſpark of grace,
  And for my hope of heavén.

3 Gracious God, my ſins forgive,
  And thy good Spirit impart,
Then I ſhall in Thee believe
  With all my loving heart,
Always unto Jeſus look,
  Him in heavénly glory ſee,
Who my cauſe hath undertook,
  And ever prays for me.

4 Grace, in anſwer to his prayér,
  And every grace beſtow,
That I may with zealous care
  Perform thy will below :
Rooted in humility,
  Still in every ſtate reſignéd,
Plant, Almighty Lord, in me
  A meek and lowly mind.

5 Poor, and vile in my own eyes,
  With ſelf-abaſing ſhame,
Still I would myſelf deſpiſe,
  And magnify thy name·
Thee let every creature bleſs,
  Praiſe to God alone be givén;
God alone deſerves the praiſe
  Of all in earth and heavén.

HYMN

H Y M N XXIII.

1 HOW ignorant the human mind,
   How totally fhut up and blind,
     Through our fiſt parents fall!
 Strangers to God by nature, we
 His things can neither know nor fee,
     But darkneſs covers all.

2 God only can our fight reſtore,
   And give us by his Spirit's power
     Spiritual things to know,
 His wiſdom, majeſty. and love,
 To view in all his works above,
     And all his works below.

3 Who good purſue, and evil fly,
   To them he grants the feeing eye,
     To them Himſelf diſplays:
 Shew then for I thy will would do)
 To me, great God, vouchſafe to ſhew,
     The wonders of thy grace.

 Open mine eyes, the veil withdraw,
 And I, O Lord, will keep thy law,
     If Thou thy light impart,
 Through grace determined to fulfil
 Thy holy, good, and perfect will,
     With all my loving heart.

H Y M N XXIV.

 TEACHER of babes to Thee,
   I for inſtruction flee ;
 In my natural eſtate,
   Thee, my God, I cannot know ;
 Let thy grace illuminate,
   Thee let thy own Spirit ſhow.

2   Ah, give me other eyes
      Than flesh and blood supplies,
Spiritual discernment give,
    Then command the light to shine,
Then I shall the truth receive,
    Know by faith the things divine.

3   For this I ever pray,
      The darkness chase away
From a foolish, feeble mind,
    Humbly offeréd up to Thee.
Help me, Lord; my soul is blind,
    Give me light, and eyes to see.

4   Thou seest my heart's desire,
      Whate'er thy laws require
Freely, faithfully to do,
    But I know not how to' obey;
Till thy Spirit lend a clue,
    Pointing out the living way.

5   Now, Father, send him down,
      To make thy Godhead known,
Let him Thee in Christ reveal,
    Now diffuse thy blood abroad,
Shew me things unsearchable,
    All the heights and depths of God.

HYMN XXV.

1 THEE, Maker of the world we praise,
    The end of our creation own,
Being thou gavést the favouréd race,
    That man might love his God alone;
With knowledge filléd, and joy, and peace,
And glorious, everlasting bliss.

2 But man his liberty of will
    Abuséd, and turnéd his heart from Thee ·
His fault on us intailed we feel,
    While born in sin and misery,

W

We from our God with horror fly,
And perifh, and for ever die.

1 3 We muft have diéd that fecond death,
  Had not the Son of God been man :
Jefus for us refignéd his breath,
  For us revivéd, and rofe again,
He purgéd our fin, he bought our peace,
And fills us with his righteoufnefs.

2 4 We now by his good Spirit led,
  Our own defires and will forego,
Delight in all his fteps to tread,
  And perfeét holinefs below,
Our ranfoméd fouls to God refign,
Filléd up with peace and joy divine.

3 5 In Jefus joinéd to God again,
  To all thy faints in earth and heavén,
We triumph with the fons of men,
  Thy utmoft grace to finners givén,
Sure at his coming to receive,
And bleft with Thee for ever live.

H Y M N XXVI.

1 FOOLISH, ignorant, and blind,
  Is finful, fhort-livéd man,
All which in the world we find
  Is perifhing and vain,
Man muft quickly turn to duft,
The world will be deftroyéd by fire;
 Who would then on either truft
  Or dotingly admire ?

2 God is good, and great alone,
  In wifdom infinite.
Let us render him his own,
  And ftill in God delight,

Fix on him our truſt, and choice,
And ſing, and wonder and adore,
In his holy will rejoice,
And triumph evermore.

HYMN XXVII.

1 COME, let us rival thoſe above,
Rejoicing in our Father's love,
Our Father is the almighty Lord,
Our Father's glorious praiſe record:
He made us to rejoice in Him,
Our firſt, and laſt, and endleſs theme.

2 Happy he doth and glorious live,
Beyond what we can e'er conceive,
He always to his promiſe ſtood,
Holy, and wiſe, and juſt, and good:
Rejoice, that God a King remains,
Rejoice that God for ever reigns.

3 Worthy is God, and God alone,
To be deſiréd, and ſought, and known:
Honour and praiſe He ſhould receive,
And bleſſing more than man can give,
And might, and majeſty, and love,
From all on earth, and all above.

4 Wherefore again we ſay rejoice,
And make to God, a cheerful noiſe,
To God who man for us became,
Extol the mighty Jeſu's name,
Who diéd to live, who ſtoopéd to riſe,
And take us with him to the ſkies.

HYMN XXVIII.

1 COVER'D with conſcious ſhame,
And grievéd, O Lord, I am,

C

Praiſe

Praife to moft unworthy me
 That my fellow worms fhould give.
Praife belongs to none but Thee,
 Praife let God alone receive.

2 Shall I, his creature I,
   By finful robbery,
 Take the honour and efteem
  To my glorious Maker due?
No, I leave it all to Him,
 Him from whom my life I drew.

3 Father, accept thine own,
   Through Jefus Chrift thy Son:
 Honour, glory, powér is thine,
  Mine (if Thou vouchfafe the grace)
With that heavénly choir to join,
 In thine everlafting praife.

H Y M N XXIX.

1 REJOICE in the Lord, Rejoice evermore!
  Who gave us the word, Shall give us the
   power:
His grace is a treafure, Which when we obtain,
Obedience is pleafure, And duty is gain.

2 The pleafure and gain Of them that believe,
The reafon of man Can never conceive.
Too big for expreffion The comfort and peace,
'Tis prefent poffeffion Of heavenly blifs.

3 Who fhare it above, They never can lofe
His heavénly love, Or forfeit, like us,
Immanuel's favour, And therefore they reft
Wrapt up in their Saviour, And perfectly bleft.

H Y M N XXX.

1 BUT we by divers ways
  May fall from Jefu's grace,

Let

Let him every moment go,
  Lose our treasure and reward ,
Watch we then against our foe,
  Stand for ever on our guard.

2　　With reverential joy
　　　Let us our time employ,
　Joy at Jesu's hands receive,
　　Tempered with a serious fear,
　Humbly, circumspectly live,
　　Sin, the world, and hell so near.

3　　Dangers and snares abound,
　　　And ever close us round,
　Numberless, malicious powers
　　Fight against us night and day,
　Satan as a lion roars,
　　Watching to devour his prey.

4　　But our almighty Lord,
　　　Shall still his help afford,
　Arm us with his patient mind,
　　Till we see our conflicts past,
　Perfect joy and safety find,
　　More than conquerors at last.

H Y M N XXXI.

Before reading the Scriptures.

1 O That I, like Timothy,
　　Might the whole scriptures know
From mine earliest infancy,
　　Till for God mature I grow,
Made unto salvation wise,
Ready for the glorious prize.

2 Jesus, all-redeeming Lord,
　　Full of truth and full of grace,
Make me understand thy word,
　　Teach me in my youthful days,

C 2

Wonders

Wonders in thy word to fee,
Wife through Faith which is in Thee.

3 Open now mine eyes of faith,
   Open now the book of God,
Shew me here the fecret path,
   Leading to thy bleft abode,
Wifdom from above impart,
Speak the meaning to my heart.

H Y M N XXXII.

1   COME let us embrace,
      In our earlieft days,
The offers of life and falvation by grace;
    Let us gladly believe,
    And the pardon receive,
Which the Father of mercies thro' Jefus doth give.

2   His kingdom below
    He hath calléd us to know,
And in ftatuie and heavénly wifdom to grow;
    In his woik to remain,
    Till his image we gain,
And the fulnefs of Chrift in perfeftion attain.

3   Then let us begin,
    By renouncing all fin,   [clean:
And expefting the blood that fhall wafh our hearts
    With endeavour fincere
    To Jefus draw near,
And be inftant in prayer till our Saviour appear.

4   If now Thou art nigh,
    Appear at our cry,
Thy love to reveal, and thy blood to apply,
    Thy little one's own,
    And perfeft in one,
And admit us at laft to a fhare of thy throne.

HYMN XXXIII.

1 HOSANNA to the Son
Of David on his throne!
Coming in Jehovah's name,
Us, and all mankind to blefs,
Let the ftammering babes proclaim,
Let the fongs of children praife.

2 Jefus will not defpife
Our meaneft facrifice:
Though by higheft heaven adoréd,
Children Thou doft ftill approve,
Suffer us to call Thee Lord,
Smile to hear us lifp thy love.

3 Saviour, thy mercy's praife
Shall take up all our days,
For this only thing we live,
Our Redeemer to commend,
Glory, thanks to thee we give,
Soon begin, but never end.

4 Thee, Lord, we hope to' adore,
When time fhall be no more:
Only keep us to the day,
When the angel-guards fhall come,
Bear us on their wings away
To our everlafting home.

HYMN XXXIV.

1 HOLY Child of heavénly birth,
God made manifeft on earth,
Fain I would thy follower be,
Live in evéry thing like Thee.

2 Thou whom angels ferve and fear,
Subject to thy parents here,

Didft

Didſt to me the pattern give,
How with mine I ought to live.

3 Teach me then betimes to' obey
Thoſe who under God bear ſway:
Maſters, miniſters to love,
All their juſt commands approve.

4 Let me to my betters bend,
Never wilfully offend,
By my meek ſubmiſſiveneſs
Strive both God and them to pleaſe.

5 Thy humility impart,
Give me thy obedient heart,
Free and cheerful to fulfil
All my heavénly Father's will.

6 Keep me thus to God reſignéd,
Till his love delights to find
Fairly copied out on me,
All the mind that was in Thee.

H Y M N   XXXV.

A Thought on Judgment.

1 AND muſt I be to judgment brought,
   And anſwer in that day
For evéry vain, or idle thought,
   And evéry word I ſay!

2 Yes, evéry ſecret of my heart
   Shall ſhortly be made known,
And I receive my juſt deſert
   For all that I have done.

3 How careful then ought I to live,
   With what religious fear,
Who ſuch a ſtrict account muſt give;
   Of my behaviour here!

4 The

4 The awful Judge of quick and dead,
 The watchful powér beſtow,
So ſhall I to my ways take heed,
 To all I ſpeak and do.

5 If now Thou ſtandeſt at the door,
 O let me feel Thee near,
And make my peace with God, before
 I at thy bar appear.

6 My peace Thou haſt already made,
 While hanging on the tree,
.My ſins He on thy body laid,
 And puniſhéd them in Thee.

7 Ah, might I, Lord, the virtue prove
 Of thine atoning blood,
And know, Thou ever livéſt above,
 My Advocate with God:

8 Receive the anſwer of thy prayér,
 The ſenſe of ſin forgivén,
And follow Thee with loving care,
 And go in peace to heavén.

H Y M N XXXVI.

1 THE Lord he knows the thoughts of men,
 That they are fooliſh all and vain,
Till chaſtenéd by affliction's rod,
The ſinners mourn, and turn to God.

2 O might his grace victorious prove,
And draw us with the cords of love,
To ſeek Him in the dawn of day,
And gladly from our hearts obey.

3 Father, the kind inſtruction give,
And let us now begin to live,
To live the life of piety,
To live like creatures born for Thee.

4 Taught

4 Taught by the Spirit of thy grace
  O may we rightly count our days,
  To wisdom's rules our hearts apply,
  And warm in life prepare to die.

5 And when our spirits we resign
  Into those gracious hands of thine,
  Thy new-born children, Lord, receive,
  With Thee eternally to live.

H Y M N XXXVII.

1 WHEN dear Lord, ah, tell us when,
    Shall we be in knowledge men,
  Men in strength and constancy,
  Men of God, confirméd in Thee?

2 Childish now alas we are,
  Void of faith and watchful care,
  After all our teachers' pains,
  Little good in us remains.

3 Soon our best desires decay,
  As a cloud they pass away,
  Light receivéd the serious thought,
  Soon, and easily forgot.

4 O how fickle is our mind,
  More inconstant than the wind,
  Suddenly our goodness fails,
  Levity again prevails.

5 Strong and fervent for an hour,
  Then we cast away the power,
  Lose insensibly our zeal,
  Care for neither heaven nor hell.

6 Jesus, Lord, we cry to Thee,
  Help our soul's infirmity,
  Great unchangeable I AM,
  Make us evermore the same.

7 Plant in us thy conſtant mind,
  To thy croſs our ſpirit bind,
  That we may no longer rove,
  Ground and ſtabliſh us in love.

8 Love that makes us creatures new,
  Only love can keep us true,
  Perfect love that caſts out ſin,
  Perfect love is God within.

9 God within our hearts reſide
  Then we ſhall in God abide,
  Always firm and faithful prove,
  Fixt in everlaſting love.

H Y M N   XXXVIII.

1 LET children proclaim Their Saviour and
      King!
  To Jeſus's name Hoſannas we ſing,
  Our beſt adoration To Jeſus we give,
  Who purchaſéd ſalvation For all to receive.

2 The meek Lamb of God From heaven came
      down,   [own;
  And ranſoméd with blood, And made us his
  He ſufferéd to lave us From ſin and from thrall,
  And Jeſus ſhall have us, Who purchaſéd us all.

3 To him will we give Our earlieſt days,
  And thankfully live, To publiſh his praiſe,
  Our lives ſhall confeſs him who came from above,
                                   [love.
  Our tongues, they ſhall bleſs him, And tell of his

4 In innocent ſongs His coming we ſhout:
  Should we hold our tongues, The ſtones would
    cry out
  But Him without ceaſing We all will proclaim,
  And ever be bleſſing Our Jeſus's name.
                                   HYMN

HYMN XXXIX.

1   O Saviour of all,
     We come at thy call,
In the morning of life at thy feet do we fall.
     Thy mercy is free ;
     Our helpleſſneſs ſee,
And let little children be brought unto thee.

2   To us thy love ſhow
     Who nothing do know,
For of ſuch is the kingdom of heavén below :
     O give us thy grace
     In our earlieſt days,
And let us grow up to thy honour and praiſe.

3   But rather than live
     Thy goodneſs to grieve,
Back into thy hands we our ſpirits would give :
     O take us away
     In the morn of our day,
And let us no longer in miſery ſtay.

4   If now we remove,
     Thy pity and love
Will certainly take us to heaven above:
     With Thee we ſhall dwell,
     Who haſt lovéd us ſo well :
For O, wilt Thou ſend little children to hell?

5   We need not come there,
     But at death may repair
To heavén, and heavénly happineſs ſhare :
     Us mercy ſhall raiſe
     To that happy place,
And we ſhall behold with our angels thy face.

6   They now are our guard,
     And ready preparéd
To carry us hence to our glorious reward ,

                   Ere

Ere long it fhall be;
We are ranfoméd by Thee,
And we our all-loving Redeemer fhall fee.

7   Our bodies are thine,
Our fouls we refign
To be wholly employéd in the fervice divine,
Our fpirits we give
For Thee to receive·
O who would not die, with his Saviour to live!

H Y M N XL.

At the opening of the School in Kingswood.

1 COME, Father, Son, and Holy Ghoft,
    To whom we for our children cry,
The good defiréd and wanted moft
    Out of thy richeft grace fupply,
The facred difcipline be givén
To train, and bring them up for heavén.

2 Anfwer on them that end of all
    Our cares, and pains and ftudies here,
On them, recoveréd from their fall,
    Stampt with the heavénly charaċter,
Raiféd by the nurture of the Lord,
To all their paradife reftoréd.

3 Error and ignorance remove,
    Their blindnefs both of heart and mind,
Give them the wifdom from above,
    Spotlefs, and peaceable, and kind;
In knowledge pure their mind renew,
And ftore with thoughts divinely true.

4 Learning's redundant part and vain
    Be here cut off and caft afide
But let them, Lord, the fubftance gain,
    In evéry folid truth abide.

Swiftly

Swiftly acquire, and ne'er forego
The knowledge fit for man to know.

5 Unite the pair so long disjoinéd,
   Knowledge and vital piety,
Learning and holinefs combinéd,
   And truth and love let all men fee
In thefe whom up to thee we give,
Thine, wholly thine to die and live.

6 Father, accept them in thy Son,
   And ever by thy Spirit guide,
Thy wifdom in their lives be fhown,
   Thy name confeffed and glorifiéd,
Thy power and love diffuféd abroad,
Till all our earth is filléd with God.

HYMN XLI.

1 CAPTAIN of our falvation, take
   The Souls we here prefent to Thee,
And fit for thy great fervice make
   Thefe heirs of immortality,
And let them in thine image rife,
And then tranfplant them to the fkies.

2 Unfpotted from the world and pure,
   Preferve them for thy glorious caufe,
Accuftoméd daily to endure
   The welcome burthen of thy crofs;
Innuréd to toil and patient pain,
Till all thy perfect mind they gain.

3 Our Sons henceforth be wholly thine,
   And ferve and love Thee all their days:
Infufe the principle divine
   In all who here expect thy grace.
Let each improve the grace beftowéd,
Rife every child a man of God!

4 Train up thy hardy foldiers, Lord,
    In all their Captain's fteps to tread,
Or fend them to proclaim thy word,
    The gofpel thro' the world to fpread,
Freely as they receive to give,
And preach the death by which they live.

H Y M N   XLII.

1 BUT who fufficient is to lead
    And execute the vaft defign?
How can our arduous toil fucceed,
    When earth and hell their forces join,
The meaneft inftruments to' o'erthrow
Which Thou haft ever ufed below?

2 Mountains alas, on mountains rife,
    To make our utmoft efforts vain,
The work our feeble ftrength defies,
    And all the helps and hopes of man,
Our utter impotence we fee;
But nothing is too hard for Thee.

3 The things impoffible to man
    Thou canft for thy own people do:
Thy ftrength be in our weaknefs feen,
    Thy wifdom in our folly fhow,
Prevent, accompany, and blefs,
And crown the whole with full fuccefs.

4 Unlefs the power of heavenly grace,
    The wifdom of the Deity
Direct, and govern all our ways,
    And all our works be wrought in Thee,
Our blafted works, we know, fhall fail,
And earth and hell at laft prevail.

5 But O, almighty God of love,
    Into thy hands the matter take,
The mountain-obftacle remove,
    For thy own truth and mercy fake;
D

Fulfil

Fulfil in ours thy own defign,
And prove the work entirely thine.

H Y M N XLIII.

1 HOW haplefs are the lettered youth,
   How diftant from the paths of truth,
      And folid happinefs!
   Their knowledge makes them doubly blind,
   The med'cine for their fin-fick mind,
      But heightens their difeafe.

2 The world's, and fin's, and Satan's prey,
   At the firft ftep they go aftray,
      Nor ever God *intend* ·
   They do not at his glory aim,
   Begin their work in Jefu's name,
      Or make his love their end.

3 By ten years fiege the fort they take,
   And learning's fhell their own they make,
      With outward knowledge fraught:
   But tutored for this world alone,
   The one thing needful to be known,
      They and their Guides forgot.

4 In fpecious pride and envy bred,
   Down a broad beaten track they tread,
      As vicious nature draws;
   With hellifh emulation fired,
   They luft to be careffed, admired,
      And pampered with applaufe.

5 Their teachers edge their thirft of fame,
   And pour more oil upon the flame,
      And raife their paffions higher,
   Like *Herod*, each the children flays,
   Or makes the helplefs victims pafs
      To *Molock* through the fire.

6 Who shall arise in their defence,
 The cause of injuréd innocence
  With genérous zeal maintain,
 Train up poor children for the Lord,
 And serve, expecting no reward,
  Till one in heavén they gain?

7 Lord, if Thou hast our hearts inclinéd,
 And for this very thing designéd
  The meanest of the crowd,
 With suitable endowments bless,
 With gifts of learning and of grace,
  To build the house of God.

8 To those Thou shalt with us entrust,
 O make us diligently just,
  With strict fidelity
 To answer all we undertake,
 And not for gain, but conscience' sake,
  To breed them up for Thee.

9 Here let thy Providence preside,
 Thy Spirit be our constant guide,
  Thy word our perfect rule,
 Their prayérs let all the faithful join,
 With truth, and power, and love divine,
  To found *The Christian School.*

10 So be it, Lord, our labours speed,
 And for thyself raise up a seed,
  Thy name to glorify;
 A generation wise and good,
 With solid piety enduéd,
  And knowledge from on high.

11 Mould them according to thy will,
 And set the city on the hill,
  The fairly rising race,
 To scatter light on all around,
 And to succeeding times resoun.
  Thine everlasting praise.

D 2

HYMN

H Y M N XLIV.

For the Scholars.

O Thou, whofe Providential grace
  Hath been in our behalf made known.
From different parts, by fecret ways,
  Whofe eye hath drawn us into one,
The things moft excellent to' approve
And learn the power of dying Love ·

2 We lift our thankful hearts to Thee,
  And gladly clofe with thy defign,
With early zeal from evil flee,
  In following after Jefus join,
And long to feel his fprinkléd blood,
And long to cry, My Lord, my God!

3 Father, to us thy Spirit give,
  Him in our youthful hearts reveal;
Him by whofe precious death we live,
  Redeeméd from fin, and earth, and hell,
Through whom our Eden we regain,
And then in heavénly glory reign.

4 Now, Lord, the gracious work begin,
  His blood to every foul apply,
Affure me of my pardonéd fin,
  Confirm, and throughly fanctify,
Prepare us for that endlefs reft,
And take thy children to thy breaft.

H Y M N XLV.

1 HOW fad our ftate by nature is,
  While enemies to God,
We wander from the way of peace,
  And throng the downward road.

2 As a wild afs's colt is man,
   Untaught and unconfinéd,
Till difcipline his will reftrain,
   And faith inform his mind.

3 But O, with what reluctant ftrife
   Do men themfelves forego!
How late begin the work of life,
   How late their Saviour know!

4 Calléd in the morning of their day,
   How few like us are bleft!
Us, if we now the call obey,
   And fly to Jefu's breaft.

5 This, Lord, is our fincere defire,
   To find our reft in Thee,
To do whate'er thy laws require
   In true fimplicity!

6 The inward change, the fecond birth,
   By faith divine to prove,
And practife all thy will on earth,
   As angels do above.

H Y M N XLVI.

1 HAPPY *Samuel*, to God
   In his infancy reftoréd!
In his Maker's houfe he ftood,
   Miniftring before the Lord:
There he livéd to God alone,
   Pure from fin's infecting ftain,
Grew in years and wifdom on,
   Favouréd both by God and man.

2 Happy Child! who gainéd a place
   To his heavénly Lord fo near!
Happier ftill, who found the grace
   God's majeftic voice to hear!

Myftéries

Myfteries hidden from the wife,
From the prudent *men* conceáled,
God, the Lord of earth and fkies,
To a fimple babe reveáled.

3 Lord of earth and fkies, again
To a child thyfelf make known,
Chofen from the fons of men,
Am not I thy facred loan?
Yes, I to thy temple come,
By my parents piety
Dedicated from the womb,
Freely given up to Thee.

4 Thine, O Lord, I furely am,
But to me unknown Thou art;
Come, and call me by my name,
Whifper to my liftening heart;
Stir me up to feek thy face,
Claim me in my tender years,
Manifeft the word of grace:
Speak, for now thy fervant hears.

5 Fain I would, I would believe,
Hear by faith thy pard'ning voice;
Of thy love the knowledge give,
Bid me, Lord, in Thee rejoice,
Now thy gracious Self reveal,
Speak in power and peace divine,
Pardon on my confcience feal,
Seal thy child for ever thine.

H Y M N XLVII.

1 FATHER, with joy we praife
Thy Providential care,
Snatchéd in our youthful days
From fin and Satan's fnare.

We

We own and thankfully approve
　　Thy merciful defign,
And vow to feek the things above,
　　And live entirely thine.

2　　　But vain our vows we know,
　　　　And ftrongeft promifes,
　　　Unlefs our God beftow,
　　　　The power himfelf to pleafe ·
Nor men, nor means can change the heart,
　　Or render it fincere,
Till Thou the principle impart,
　　Of godly, gracious fear.

3　　　Hear then thy children's call,
　　　　Fulfil thy own defire,
　　　And kindle in us all
　　　　A fpark of heavénly fire,
A tafte of God, a feed of grace
　　Let evéry foul receive,
And now begin the Chriftian race,
　　And now begin to live.

4　　　Trainéd up in the true way
　　　　Wherein we ought to go,
　　　Preferve us, left we ftray,
　　　　When more in years we grow :
O let us not, when old, depart
　　From our integrity,
But love our God with all our heart,
　　And live and die to Thee.

H Y M N　XLVIII.

1　HOW wretched are the boys at fchool,
　　　Who wickedly delight
To mock, and call each other fool,
　　And with each other fight!

2 Who foon their innocency lofe,
  And learn to curfe and fwear.
Or, if they do no harm, fuppofe
  That good enough they are.

3 O how much happier we than they!
  We from the paths of vice
Removéd far off, and taught the way
  That leads us to the fkies!

4 We to the Lamb's atoning blood
  Are pointed in our youth,
And rightly taught to worfhip God
  In fpirit and in truth.

5 Yet nought have we whereof to boaft,
  As wifer than the reft,
He is not wife who knows the moft,
  But he who lives the beft.

6 If God on us hath much beftowéd,
  He will require the more:
We ought to ferve and love our God
  With all our heart and powér.

7 But if we live in vice and fin,
  And make him no return,
Far better it for us had been
  That we had ne'er been born.

8 We fhall with many ftripes be beat,
  The foreft judgment feel,
And of all wicked children meet
  The hotteft place in hell.

H Y M N XLIX.

1 BUT O, we hope for better things:
  Who left his throne above,
We truft, fhall hide us with his wings,
  And wrap us in his love.

2 He who fo much for us hath done,
    Will ftill our fouls defend,
And carry on the work begun,
    To a triumphant end.

3 Guide of our weak, unftable youth,
    Jefu, thy fpirit give,
To lead into all faving truth
    Us who thy grace receive.

4 We do with thanks receive it now,
    To keep with humble care,
And all our necks and fpirits bow
    Thine eafy yoke to bear.

5 To Thee our ftedfaft hearts fhall cleave
    In thefe our earlieft days,
Thee whom we long to ferve, and live,
    To fpread abroad thy praife.

6 Out of our mouth and life, O Lord,
    Thy perfect praife ordain :
And let us live to keep thy word,
    And die with Thee to reign.

H Y M N L.

1 HOW happy, Lord, thy children are,
    Far from the world and all its care,
        And all its fins removéd,
Thou doft for us a place provide,
And in the fecret defert hide,
        And nour'fh thy Belovéd.

2 Hither by fpecial mercy led,
    A little flock, a chofen feed,
        We fhun the paths of men ;
Calléd in our confecrated youth,
To liften for the voice of truth,
        And folid learning gain.

3 Thou callést us here to feek thy face,
 To learn the leſſons of thy grace,
  And feel the atoning blood ·
 Thou talkéft to every heart fincere,
 That all thy paid'ning voice may hear,
  And find Thee in the wood.

4 Come then the Life, the Truth, the Way,
 Now in the morning of our day,
  Thefe clouds of fin remove,
 Make us unto falvation wife,
 And help us to fecure the prize
  Of thy eternal love.

H Y M N LI.

1   O For a thankful heart,
   Our Father's love to own,
 To tafte how merciful thou art
  In all that Thou haft done!
  How bountiful and kind
   To us above the reft,
 If bleft with a contented mind,
  We know that we are bleft.

2   Thy Providence hath caréd,
   For our fimplicity,
 For us a place and means preparéd
  Of rightly knowing Thee:
  To glorify thy name,
   Us Thou haft hither led,
 To ferve and love the bleeding Lamb,
  Who fufferéd in our ftead.

3   Ah, let us not receive,
   Thy choiceft grace in vain,
 Nor ever more thy fpirit grieve,
  Or put our Lord to pain!

Lightnefs

Lightnefs and difcontent,
With evéry fin depart,
And let us each to Thee prefent
A willing, honeft heart.

4   Lord, we prefent it now,
For thee to form anew,
Our Maker and Redeemer Thou,
Thine utmoft pleafure fhew;
In us with powér fulfil
The work of faith divine,
And take us to thy heavénly hill,
To live for ever thine.

H Y M N LII.

Before School.

1 FATHER, to Thee our foul's we raife,
And for a bleffing look,
Prevent, and help us by thy grace
In learning of our book.

2 Give us an humble, active mind,
From floth and folly free,
Give us a cheerful heart, inclinéd
To truth and piety.

3 A faithful memory beftow,
With folid learning ftore,
And ftill, O Lord, as more we know,
Let us obey Thee more.

4 Let us things excellent difcern,
Hold faft what we approve,
And above all delight to learn,
The leffons of thy love.

HYMN

H Y M N LIII.

In School.

1 STILL let us keep the end in mind
    For which we hither came,
In ſearch of uſeful knowledge joinéd,
    As followérs of the Lamb.

2 Thro' Him let us to God look up
    In evéry ſtep we take,
And for his conſtant bleſſing hope,
    For Jeſu's only ſake.

3 His grace, if God on us confer,
    We then ſhall learn apace,
Live to his glory and declare,
    Our heavénly Teacher's praiſe.

4 We in his favour ſhall retrieve
    Our long loſt paradiſe,
Take of the Tree of Life, and live
    Immortal in the ſkies.

H Y M N LIV.

After School.

1 JESUS, we caſt ourſelves on Thee,
    On Thee our works we caſt,
The Alpha and Omega be,
    In all, the firſt and laſt.

2 If well we any thing have done,
    'Tis owing to thy grace
What therefore we with praiſe begun,
    We now conclude with praiſe.

3 We praiſe Thee for our Maſter's care,
    To us poor children ſhowéd,
If forward brought to day we are,
    It is the gift of God.

4 We praife Thee for our hope to know
   The wifdom from above,
And own that all our bleffings flow
   From thy expiring love.

H Y M N LV.

Againft Idlenefs.

1 IDLE boys and men are found,
   Standing on the devil's ground,
He will find them work to do,
He will pay their wages too.

2 Are they not of wifdom void,
   Thofe that faunter unemployéd,
Young, or old, who fondly play
Their important time away?

3 What a bold and foolifh lye,
   When we hear a trifler cry,
" I no other bufinefs have!"
Has he not a foul to fave?

4 Has he from his Lord above,
   No one talent to improve?
Let him go and mufe on this,
Sloth is the worft wickednefs.

5 Sloth is the accurfed root,
   Whence ten thoufand evils fhoot,
Evéry vice and evéry fin,
Doth with idlenefs begin.

6 We by idlenefs expofe
   Our own fouls to endlefs woes,
We, whenever loitéring thus,
Tempt the devil to tempt us.

7 But fuffice the feafon paft,
   That our time away we caft,
Thoughtlefs and infenfible,
Dancing on the brink of hell.

E   8 Let

8 Let us now to Jefus turn,
   For our mif-fpent moments mourn,
   Let us in his Spirit's powér
   Promife to ftand ftill no more.

9 Jefus help; to Thee we pray,
   Take the curfed root away,
   Idlenefs far off remove,
   Let us Thee and labour love;

10 All our time and vigour give,
    Serve our Maker while we live,
    Ufe for God the talents givén,
    Work on earth, and reft in heavén.

H Y M N LVI.

Againft Lying.

1 HAPPY the well-inftructed youth
     Who in his earliéft infancy,
   Loves from his heart to fpeak the truth,
     And like his God abhors a lye.

2 He that has practiféd no deceit
     With falfe equivocating tongue,
   Nor evén durft o'er-reach, or cheat,
     Or flandéroufly his neighbour wrong:

3 He in the houfe of God fhall dwell,
     He on his holy hill fhall reft,
   The comforts of religion feel,
     And then be numberéd with the bleft.

4 But who or guile or falfehood ufe,
     Or take God's name in vain, or fwear,
   Or ever lye themfelves to' excufe,
     They fhall their dreadful fentence bear.

5 The Lord, the true and faithful Lord,
     Himfelf hath faid, that evéry lyar,
   Shall furely meet his juft reward,
     Affignéd him in eternal fire.

HYMN

H Y M N LVII.

1 O May I to my ways take heed,
    Nor ever with my tongue offend,
Or grieve that God by word or deed,
    Whose wrath can punish without end!

2 O may I never, never tell,
    To gain the world, one wilful lye,
For what would the whole world avail,
    If my own soul I loft thereby?

3 Thou, Lord, who art the Truth, the Way,
    On me the saving grace beftow,
─ To keep me, left I go aftray,
    To make me in thy footfteps go.

4 Still may I in the truth delight,
    Still may I take delight in Thee,
Order my converfation right,
    And all thy great falvation fee.

5 So fhall I fee thy face with joy,
    When caught up to thy throne above,
And all eternity employ
    In praifes of thy faithful love.

H Y M N LVIII.

1 WHY fhould our parents call us good,
    And poifon us with praife,
When born in fin by nature proud,
    And void we are of grace?

2 Who fancy righteoufnefs in man,
    Themfelves they have not known,
Evil are all our thoughts and vain,
    And God is good alone.

E 2

3 Good

3 Good of himfelf He only is;
    And if he makes us good,
Our goodnefs is not ours, but his,
    For Jefu's fake beftowéd.

4 O let us not ourfelves forget,
    Tho' man prefume to praife,
And puff us up with the conceit
    Of our own righteoufnefs.

5 O let us as from ferpents fly
    From all who us commend,
Or filléd with juft abhorrence cry,
    Get thee behind me, fiend!

6 Glory to God, if we receive
    The fmalleft fpark of grace,
He only doth our goodnefs give,
    And his be all the praife.

HYMN LIX.

1   AND am I born to die,
    To lay this body down?
And muft my trembling fpirit fly
    Into a world unknown?
    A world of darkeft fhade,
    Unpiercéd by human thought,
The dreary regions of the dead,
    Where all things are forgot!

2   Soon as from earth I go,
    What will become of me?
Eternal happinefs or woe
    Muft then my portion be:
    Wakéd by the trumpet's found
    I from my grave fhall rife,
And fee the Judge with glory crownéd,
    And fee the flaming fkies.

3 How

'3   How fhall I leave my tomb?
        With triumph, or regret?
A fearful, or a joyful doom,
        A curfe, or bleffing meet?
        Shall angel-bands convey
        Their brother to the bar?
Or devils drag my foul away,
        To meet its fentence there?

4   Who can refolve the doubt
        That tears my anxious breaft?
Shall I be with the damned caft out?
        Or numberéd with the bleft?
        I muft from God be driven,
        Or with my Saviour dwell,
Muft come, at his command, to heaven,
        Or elfe depart to hell.

5   O Thou who wouldéft not have
        One wretched finner die,
Who diédft thyfelf my foul to fave
        From endlefs mifery,
        Shew me the way to fhun
        Thy dreadful wrath fevere,
That when Thou comeft on thy throne,
        I may with joy appear.

6   Thou art thyfelf the way:
        Thyfelf in me reveal,
So fhall I pafs my life's fhort day,
        Obedient to thy will:
        So fhall I love my God,
        Becaufe he firft lovéd me,
And praife Thee in thy bright abode,
        Thro' all eternity.

          HYMN

H Y M N LX.

A Thought on Hell.

1 TERRIBLE thought! fhall I alone,
    Who may be favéd, fhall I
Of all alas, whom I have known,
    Thro' fin for ever die?

2 While all my old companions dear,
    With whom I once did live,
Joyful at God's right-hand appear,
    A blefling to receive;

3 Shall I, amidft a ghaftly band
    Draggéd to the judgment-feat,
Far on the left with horror ftand,
    My fearful doom to meet?

4 Abandonéd to extreme defpair,
    Eternally undone,
My Father would not own me there,
    His hell-devoted fon.

5 Diffolvéd are nature's clofeft ties,
    And bofom-friends forgot,
When God, the juft Avenger, cries
    Depart, I know you not.

6 But muft I from his glorious face,
    From all his faints retire?
But muft I go to my own place,
    In everlafting fire?

7 While they enjoy his heavénly love,
    Muft I in torments dwell,
And howl (while they fing hymns above)
    And blow the flames of hell?

8 Ah, no. I ftill may turn and live,
    For ftill his wrath delays,
He now vouchfafes a kind reprieve,
    And offers me his grace.

9 I *will* accept his offers now,
 From evéry fin depart,
 Perform my oft-repeated vow,
 And render him my heart.

10 I will improve what I receive,
 The grace through Jefus givén,
 Sure, if with God on earth I live,
 To live with God in heavén.

H Y M N LXI.

For the Lord's Day.

1 COME, let us with our Lord arife,
 Our Lord who made both earth and fkies,
 Who diéd to fave the world he made,
 And rofe triumphant from the dead :
 He rofe, the Prince of life and peace,
 And ftampéd the day for ever his.

2 This is the day the Lord hath made,
 That all may fee his powér difplayéd,
 May feel his refurrection's powér,
 And rife again to fall no more,
 In perfect rightéoufnefs renewéd,
 And filléd with all the life of God.

3 Then let us render Him his own,
 With folemn prayér approach the throne,
 With meeknefs hear the gofpel-word,
 With thanks his dying love record,
 Our joyful hearts and voices raife,
 And fill his courts with fongs of praife.

4 Honour and praife to Jefus pay,
 Throughout his confecrated day,
 Be all in Jefu's praife employéd,
 Nor leave a fingle moment void,
 With utmoft care the time improve,
 And only breathe his praife and love.

HYMN

H Y M N LXII.

On the fame.

1 COME, let us join with one accord,
  In hymns about the throne !
This is the day our rifing Lord
  Hath made and calléd his own.

2 This is the day which God hath bleft,
  The brighteft of the feven,
Type of that everlafting reft
  The faints enjoy in heavén.

3 Then let us in his name fing on,
  And haften to that day,
When our Redeem.er fhall come down,
  And fhadows pafs away.

4 Not one, but all our days below,
  Let us in hymns employ,
And in our Lord, rejoicing go
  To his eternal joy.

H Y M N LXIII.

1 O Father of all,
  The great and the fmall,
The old and the young,
Thankfgiving accept from a ftammerer's tongue :
  Thy goodnefs we praife,
  Which has found us a place,
  Has planted us here,
To be mildly brought up in thy nurture and fear.

2   Thy mercy and truth
  In the days of our youth
  We learn to adore,
And gladly acknowledge thy wifdom and powér:
           Thy

Thy aftonifhing plan
To recover loft man,
With the heavénly quire,
We are taught in the morning of life to admire.

3 Thy favour we find
In the Friend of mankind,
Sent down from above,
The Witnefs and proof of thy fatherly love:
With joy we embrace
Thy tenders of grace,
Through the blood of the Lamb,
And accept our falvation in Jefus's name.

4 Thy mercy hath brought
Salvation unfought,
To us, and to all,
And all may be favéd, if they follow the call:
We follow it here,
Till the Saviour appear,
His faints to approve,
And carry us up to his kingdom above.

H Y M N LXIV.

1 AND am I only born to die?
And muft I fuddenly comply
With nature's ftern decree?
What after death for me remains?
Celeftial joys, or hellifh pains
Through all eternity.

2 How then ought I on earth to live,
While God prolongs the kind reprieve,
And props the houfe of clay!
My fole concein, my fingle care,
To watch, and tremble, and prepare
Againft the fatal day.

3 No room for mirth or trifling here,
  For worldly hope, or worldly fear,
    If life so soon is gone,
  If now the Judge is at the door,
  And all mankind must stand before
    The inexorable throne.

4 No matter which my thoughts employ,
  A moment's misery or joy.
    But O, when both shall end,
  Where shall I find my destined place ?
  Must I my everlasting days
    With fiends or angels spend ?

5 Nothing is worth a thought beneath,
  But how I may escape the death
    That never, never dies;
  How make my own election sure,
  And when I fail on earth, secure
    A mansion in the skies.

6 Jesus, vouchsafe a pitying ray,
  Be Thou my strength, be Thou my way
    To glorious happiness,
  Ah, write the pardon on my heart,
  And whensoe'er I hence depart,
    Let me depart in peace.

H Y M N LXV.

1   YOUNG men and maidens raise
     Your tuneful voices high,
  Old men and children, praise
    The Lord of earth and sky,
  Him three in one, and one in three
    Extol to all eternity.

2   The universal King
     Let all the world proclaim,
  Let every creature sing
    His attributes and name,
  Him three in one, and one in three
    Extol to all eternity.

3 In his great name alone
  All excellencies meet,
 Who fits upon the throne,
  And fhall for ever fit;
Him three in one, and one in three,
 Extol to all eternity.

4 Glory to God belongs,
   Glory to God be givén,
  Above the noblest fongs
   Of all in earth and heavén:
Him three in one, and one in three
 Extol to all eternity.

H Y M N   LXVI.

Before, or in their Work.

1 LET heathenifh boys
  In their paftimes rejoice,
And be foolifhly happy at play:
 Overftockéd if *they* are,
 We have nothing to fpare,
Not a moment to trifle away.

2 Our minds to unbend,
  We need not offend,
Or our Saviour by idlenefs grieve,
  Whatfoever we do,
  Our end is in view,
And to Jefus' his glory we live.

3 Recreation of mind
  We in exercife find,
And our bodily ftrength is renewéd:
  New employment is eafe,
  And our pleafure, to pleafe
By our labour a merciful God.

4 Our hearts and our hands
  He juftly demands,

And

And both to our Lord we refign;
Overpaid if He fmile
On our innocent toil,
And accept as a fervice divine.

5   In our ufeful employ
We his bleffing enjoy,
Whether clearing, or digging the ground,
With our fongs we proclaim,
Our Immanuel's name,
And our angels attend to the found.

6   The meadow and field
True pleafure doth yield,
When to either with Jefus we go;
Or a paradife find,
Like the head of mankind,
And our pains on a garden beftow.

7   Howfoever employéd
In the prefence of God,
We our forfeited Eden regain,
And delightfully rife
To our Lord in the fkies,
In his fulnefs of glory to reign.

✳✳✳✳✳✳✳✳ ✳✳✳✳✳✳✳✳

HYMNS for GIRLS.

HYMN LXVII.

1 AH! dire effect of female pride!
How deep our mother's fin, and wide,
Through all her daughters fpread!
Since firft fhe pluckéd the mortal tree,
Each woman would a goddefs be
In her Creator's ftead.

2 This fatal vanity of mind,
A curfe entailéd on all the kind,

Her

Her legacy we feel,
We neither can deny nor tame,
Our inbred eagerness for fame,
And stubbornness of will.

3 The poison spreads throughout our veins,
In all our sex the evil reigns,
The arrogant offence,
In vain we strive the plague to hide;
Our fig-leaves but bewray our pride,
And loss of innocence.

4 Deeper we sink, and deeper still,
In pride instructed and self-will,
As custom leads the way,
The world their infant charge receive,
To pleasure our young hearts we give,
And bow to passion's sway.

5 By folly taught, by nature led,
In sensual delicacy bred,
In soft luxurious ease.
A feeble mind and body meet,
And pride, and ignorance compleat
Our total uselessness.

Part the Second.

1 SEE from the world's politest school,
The goddess rise, mankind to rule,
As born for her alone!
Unclogged by thought, she issues forth,
And justly conscious of her worth,
Ascends her gaudy throne.

2 With lust of fame and pleasure fired,
The virgin shines caressed, admired,
And idolized by all
Obedient to her dread command,
Around her throne the votaries stand,
Or at her footstool fall

F

3 Prostra'e

3 Proftrate before the idol's fhrine,
  They celebrate her charms divine,
    Her beauty's awful pow'r,
  By brutal appetite infpired,
  By paffion urged, by Satan hired
    To damn whom they adore.

4 Eager fhe drinks their praifes in,
  Repeats the heaven-invading fin,
    And feems with God to dwell,
  Triumphant, till her hour is paft,
  And quite undeified at laft,
    The finner finks to hell.

Part the Third.

1 HOW highly favoured then are we,
     Snatched from a world of vanity,
    And called in Jefu's name,
  To cultivate our tender mind,
  And peace and happinefs to find,
    With the atoning Lamb!

2 Our fouls to God devoted are,
  And afk, and have our chiefeft care,
    To fafhion and improve,
  The only ornament we feek,
  A fpirit calm, and mild, and meek,
    And rich in faith and love.

3 The one thing needful we purfue,
  And when we gain the prize in view,
    And when we faith receive ;
  Still we renew the glorious ftrife,
  And trampling down the pride of life,
    To God alone we live.

  Clothed with humility and grace,
  Regardlefs of the fallen race,
    In angels eyes we fhine,
  A robe of righteoufnefs we wear,
  Than gold and pearls more precious far,
    And bought with blood divine.

5 By

5 By God approvéd, by man unknown,
The conquest of ourfelves alone,
   We zealoufly defire,
The praife defcending from above,
And none but our Redeemer's love,
   Our panting hearts require.

6 We for no worldly pleafures plead,
No innocent diverfions need,
   As Satan calls his joys:
His rattles let the tempter keep,
Or his own children rock to fleep
   With fuch amufing toys.

7 The Lord himfelf our portion is,
Unfading joy and folid blifs,
   We find with Jefus givén
We find, reclining on his breaft,
Our prefent and eternal reft,
   Our all in earth and heaven.

HYMN LXVIII.

Primitive Chriftianity.

1 THE Chriftians of old, United in one,
   As fheep in a fold, Were never alone,
As birds of a feather, They flockéd to their neft,
And fheltere'd together, In Jefus's breaft.

2 However employéd, Their joy was the fame,
They never were cloyéd, With hymning the Lamb:
Their fole recreation To fing of his praife,
And publifh falvation By Jefus's grace.

3 Small learning they had, And wanted no more:
Not many could read, But all could adore:
No help from the college Or fchool they receivéd,
Content with his knowledge In whom they be-
lievéd.

F 2   4 No

4 No riches had they But riches of grace,
   No fondnefs for play, Or paffion for praife ;
   No moments of leifure For trifling employs,
   Poffeft of the pleafure In God to rejoice.

5 Men in their own eyes Were children again,
   And children were wife And folid as men :
   The women were fearful Of nothing but fin :
   Their hearts were all cheerful, Their confciences
      clean.

6 Wrapt up in their Lord, His fervice and love,
   They livéd and adoréd, Like angels above,
   To keep in his favour, Their lives they laid down,
   And now with their Saviour Inherit the crown.

Part the Second.

1 O Where are the men With virtue endowéd,
   To live, as did then The fervants of God !
   The ancient example, Who fhews us again,
   Courageous to trample On pleafure and pain ?

2 O Jefus, on us The bleffing beftow,
   Our infancy chufe, Thy glory to fhow ;
   In this generation Thy witneffes raife,
   The heirs of falvation, The veffels of grace.

3 Accept our defire, And give us thy love,
   Thy children infpire With faith from above :
   Purge out the old leaven, And early convert,
   And open a heaven Of grace in our heart.

4 Begotten again, And principléd right,
   Good works to maintain, And walk in thy fight ;
   We then fhall recover That vigour of grace,
   And gladly live over Thofe primitive days

5 Our moments below Shall pleafantly glide,
   While nothing we know But Chrift crucifiéd,
                      Our

Our whole converſation In ſongs ſhall approve
Thy wonderful paſſion, Thy ranſoming love.

6 And if we muſt win The crown like our God,
And ſtrive againſt ſin, Reſiſting to blood ,
We more than victorious O'er death ſhall ariſe,
All happy and glorious, With Chriſt in the ſkies.

***

HYMNS for the YOUNGEST.

HYMN LXIX.

1 GENTLE Jeſus, meek and mild,
  Look upon a little child,
Pity my ſimplicity,
Suffer me to come to Thee:

2 Fain I would to Thee be brought,
Deareſt God, forbid it not .
Give me. deareſt God, a place,
In the kingdom of thy grace.

3 Put thy hands upon my head,
Let me in thine arms be ſtayéd,
Let me lean upon thy breaſt,
Lull me, lull me, Lord to reſt.

4 Hold me faſt in thine embrace,
Let me ſee thy ſmiling face,
Give me, Lord, thy bleſſing give,
Pray for me, and I ſhall live.

5 I ſhall live the ſimple life,
Free from ſin's uneaſy ſtrife,
Sweetly ignorant of ill,
Innocent and happy ſtill.

6 O that I may never know,
What the wicked people do !
Sin is contrary to Thee,
Sin is the forbidden Tree.

F 3

7 Keep

7 Keep me from the great offence,
　Guard my helplefs innocence,
　Hide me from all evil hide,
　Self, and ftubbornnefs and pride.

Part the Second.

1 LAMB of God, I look to Thee,
　　Thou fhalt my example be,
　Thou art gentle, meek, and mild,
　Thou waft once a little child.

2 Fain I would be as Thou art,
　Give me thy obedient heart;
　Thou art pitiful and kind,
　Let me have thy loving mind.

3 Meek, and lowly may I be,
　Thou art all humility ;
　Let me to my betters bow,
　Subject to thy parents Thou.

4 Let me above all fulfil
　God my heavénly Father's will,
　Never his good Spirit grieve,
　Only to his glory live.

5 Thou didft live to God alone,
　Thou didft never feek thine own,
　Thou thyfelf didft never pleafe,
　God was all thy happinefs.

6 Loving Jefus, gentle Lamb,
　In thy gracious hands I am,
　Make me, Saviour, what Thou art,
　Live thyfelf within my heart.

7 I fhall then fhew forth thy praife,
　Serve thee all my happy days,
　Then the world fhall always fee
　Chrift, the holy child in me.

HYMN

H Y M N LXX.

1 LAMB of God, I fain would be
   A meek follower of Thee,
Gentle, tractable, and mild,
Loving as a little child.

2 Simple, ignorant of ill,
   Guided by another's will,
   Trusting him for heavenly food,
   Casting all my care on God.

3 Let me in thy footsteps tread,
   Be to all the creatures dead,
   Dead to pleasure, wealth, and praise,
   Poor, and humble all my days.

4 Prepossess my tender mind,
   Let me cast the world behind,
   All its pomps and pleasures vain,
   Help me, Saviour to disdain.

5 Thou my better portion art,
   Earth shall never share my heart,
   I on all its goods look down,
   I expect a starry crown.

6 I aspire to things above,
   Lord, I give Thee all my love,
   I will nothing know beside,
   Jesus, and him crucified.

Part the Second.

1 LET the potsherds of the earth,
   Boast their virtue, beauty, birth,
A poor, guilty worm I am,
Ransoméd by the bleeding Lamb.

2 Jesus, this be all my boast,
   Thou hast savéd a sinner lost,

Thou haſt ſpilt thy ſacred blood,
Me to make a child of God.

3 What a glorious title this,
Title to eternal bliſs,
Thou for me thy life haſt givén,
Me to make an heir of heavén.

4 O enlarge my ſcanty thought,
To conceive what Thou haſt wrought,
Raiſe my grovélling ſpirit up,
To my heavénly calling's hope.

5 Greaten my contracted mind,
Saviour Thou of all mankind;
What in man thy grace could move?
O the riches of thy love!

6 Let thy love poſſeſs me whole,
Let it take up all my ſoul,
True magnificence impart,
Purify, and fill my heart.

7 I deſpiſe all earthly things,
Offspring to the King of kings,
God, I for my Father claim,
Jeſus is my brother's name.

8 Heavén is mine inheritance,
I ſhall ſoon remove from hence,
As the ſtars in glory ſhine:
Chriſt, and God, and all is mine!

H Y M N LXXI.

1 COME let us join the hoſts above,
Now in our youngeſt days,
Remember our Creator's love,
And liſp our Father's praiſe.

2 His Majeſty will not deſpiſe
The day of feeble things
Grateful the ſongs of children riſe,
And pleaſe the King of kings.

3 We all his kind protection share,
    Within his arms we rest ·
The sucklings are his tenderest care,
    While hanging on the breast.

4 We praise him with a stammering tongue,
    While under his defence,
He smiles to hear the artless song,
    Of childish innocence.

5 He loves to be remembered thus,
    And honoured for his grace,
Out of the mouth of babes like us,
    His wisdom perfects praise.

6 Glory to God, and praise, and power,
    Honour and thanks be given,
Children, and Cherubim, adore
    The Lord of earth and heaven !

H Y M N   LXXII.

1 O Happy state of infancy !
    Strangers to guilty fears,
We live from sin and sorrow free,
    In these our tender years.

2 Jesus the Lord, our Shepherd is,
    And did our souls redeem,
Our present and eternal bliss,
    Are both secured in Him.

3 His mercy every sinner claims;
    For all his flock he cares,
The sheep he gently leads, the lambs
    He in his bosom bears.

4 Loving he is to all his sons,
    Who hearken to his call,
But us, his weak, his little ones,
    He loves us best of all.

5 If unto us our friends are good,
    'Twas he their hearts inclin'd,
He bids our fathers give us food,
    And makes our mothers kind.

6 Then let us thank him for his grace,
    He will not difapprove
Our meaneſt facrifice of praiſe,
    Our childiſh prattling love.

H Y M N   LXXIII.

1 COME let us our good God proclaim
    By earth and heaven adored,
Children are bid to praiſe his name,
    And magnify the Lord.

2 Let us with all his faints agree,
    With all is hoſts above ;
Part of his family are we,
    His family of love.

3 Worthleſs are our beſt offerings,
    Our fongs are void of art,
Yet God accepts the fmalleſt things,
    Given with a willing heart.

4 Us for the fake of Chriſt he loves
    Who did our fouls redeem,
And all our childiſh thoughts approves,
    When offered up thro' him.

5 He makes us his peculiar care;
    While by his Spirit led,
We all his genuine children are,
    And on his bounty feed.

6 Though men defpife our infancy,
    Angels attend our ways,
On us they wait, yet always fee
    Our heavenly Father's face.

7 Surrounded

7 Surrounded by a flaming hoft,
  The bright Cherubic powers:
Not all the kings of earth can boaft
  Of fuch a guard as ours.

8 And while the angelic army fings,
  With them we feebly join,
To' extol the glorious King of kings,
  The Majefty Divine.

H Y M N LXXIV.

1 LOVER of little children, Thee,
    O Jefus, we adore:
  Our kind and loving Saviour be,
    Both now and evermore.

2 O take us up into thine arms,
    And we are truly bleft,
  Thy new-born babes are fafe from harms,
    While harboured in thy breaft.

3 There let us ever, ever fleep,
    Strangers to guilt and care,
  Free from the world of evil keep
    Our tender fpirits there.

4 Still as we grow in years, in grace
    And wifdom let us grow,
  But never leave thy dear embrace,
    But never evil know.

5 Strong let us in thy grace abide,
    But ignorant of ill,
  In malice, fubtlety and pride,
    Let us be children ftill.

6 Lover of little children, Thee,
    O Jefus, we adore,
  Our kind and loving Saviour be,
    Both now and evermore.

HYMN

H Y M N   LXXV.

1 JESUS, Son of David, hear,
  Thou whom angels glorify,
Blefs thine infant-worfhipper,
  Me who now Hofanna cry,
Hardly underftand the word,
  Yet I humbly pray for grace,
Teach my heart to call Thee Lord,
  Teach my heart to mean thy praife.

2 Me, they fay, thy hands have made,
  Me, thy precious blood hath bought :
But without thy Spirit's aid,
  This furpaffes all my thought :
Saviour, to my heart explain,
  Maker both of earth and fky,
How could God become a man ?
  How could God for finners die ?

3 Take me young into thy fchool,
  Me, in my fimplicity,
By the word and Spirit rule,
  Thou my kind inftructor be :
Then I fhall my Mafter prize,
  Then I fhall my Saviour love,
Till on angels wings I rife,
  Rife, and fing thy praife above.

H Y M N   LXXVI.

For the Morning.

1 FATHER, I wake thy love to praife,
  Which hath my weaknefs kept,
Thy mercy did the angels place,
  To guard me while I flept.

2 I laid me down in peace, and rife
  Thy goodnefs to proclaim,
Prefent my morning facrifice,
  My thanks in Jefu's name.

3 Becaufe

3 Because he bought me with his blood,
    Into thy favour take,
And still be merciful and good
    To me for Jesu's sake.

4 Throughout this day thy mercy show,
    And still thy child defend,
Till all my spotless life below
    In heavenly glories end.

HYMN LXXVII.

For the Evening.

1 SAVIOUR, Thou hast bestowed on me
    The blessing of the light,
And wilt my kind Preserver be
    Through this approaching night:

2 Evil from me far off remove,
    That with thy favour blest,
Beneath the shadow of thy love
    I in thine arms may rest.

3 Thy gracious eye which never sleeps
    Is always fixt on man,
Thy love the slumbering children keeps
    From sorrow, fear, and pain.

4 Wherefore I safely lay me down,
    And trust myself to Thee,
The Father's well-beloved Son,
    Who ever prayest for me.

HYMN LXXVIII.

1 HOSANNA to Him who ruleth on high!
    A world to redeem, He came from the sky;
The Almighty Creator (O how could it be?)
Appeared in our nature, An infant like me.

2 Who all the bright train Angelical made,
Subjected to man, His parents obeyed,
On sinners attended, Their minister was,
And patiently ended His life on a cross.

G   3 O how

3 O how fhall I praife Thy wonderful love?
　　Thy fpirit of grace Send down from above;
　If ftill the dear Lover Of children Thou art,
　My Saviour, difcover Thyfelf to my heart.

H Y M N LXXIX.

1 THE children in their earlieft days
　　To Jefus brought, are truly bleft:
　He folds them in his kind embrace,
　　He warms them in his tender breaft.

2 One of thofe happy children, me
　　Saviour, into thy arms receive,
　Brought by my parents prayers to Thee,
　　O may I in thy kingdom live.

3 They tell me Thou art good indeed,
　　And wouldéft to all thy grace impart;
　Put then thy hands upon my head,
　　Put faith into my fimple heart.

4 Thee may I for my portion chufe,
　　To Thee through life obedient prove,
　And now obtain, and never lofe
　　The bleffing of my Saviour's love.

H Y M N LXXX.

1 JESUS his own difciples chid,
　　Who out of falfe efteem,
　The parents foolifhly forbid
　　That brought their babes to him.

2 Methinks even now I hear him fay
　　In fervent charity,
　I will not have them kept away,
　　Bring all your babes to Me.

3 Though men our fimplenefs defpife,
　　Our Saviour doth maintain
　They muft be fmall in their own eyes,
　　If they with us would reign.

4 To

4 To little ones, and not to men,
    Is grace and glory given,
Children they muſt become again,
    Or never enter heaven.

H Y M N LXXXI.

1 THEE, Jeſus, the Son
    Of *David* I own,
By all heaven adored,   [I ord,
Thou art come from above, in the name of the
    To the houſe I repair
    Of thankſgiving and prayer,
    With the children draw nigh,
And loud in the temple hoſanna, I cry.

2   In my earlieſt hour
    I acknowledge thy power,
    Thy wiſdom approve,
And am taught by my parents to pray for thy love:
    Thee, an infant of days
    With wonder I praiſe,
    Thee the God over all
I confeſs, and on Thee for ſalvation I call.

3   Let mercy attend,
    My ſoul to defend
    From offences and ſins,
While I ſcarcely can tell what iniquity means ;
    But deliver thine own
    From the evil unknown,
    And aſſiſt me to cry,
" Let me live to be good, or in innocence die !"

H Y M N LXXXII.

1 ALL glory to God,
    Who on man hath beſtowéd
The unſpeakable gift of his Son !
    Little children we ſing
    At the birth of a king,
Who will give us a ſhare of his throne.

2   His aſtoniſhing birth,
Brings peace upon earth,
And praiſe to his Father above,
Who is now reconciléd
By that innocent Child,
And his anger is turnéd into love.

3   For Immanuel's ſake,
Who our nature did take,
He is pleaſéd with the children of men;
And if Chriſt we believe,
Will his rebels receive
To the arms of his mercy again.

4   By the Spirit of grace,
We our Saviour embrace,
And expeɛt he again will come down,
Our ſouls to remove
By the powér of his love,
And with heavénly glory to crown.

H Y M N LXXXIII.

THOU whom angel-quires proclaim,
Haſt bid the children chaunt thy name;
Loofen then the ſtamméring tongue,
Liſten to my artleſs ſong:
Now my infant voice I raiſe,
Liſp an unknown Saviour's praiſe;
And feebly thus begin to ſing
Under the ſhadow of thy wing.

H Y M N LXXXIV.

LORD, that I may ſing to Thee,
And make the ſweeteſt melody,
Bid my ſoul in hymns aſpire,
Echo to the Pſalmiſt's lyre,
Tune my heart to praiſe the Lamb,
(Jeſus his harmonious name)
And when Thou doſt from earth remove,
Give me a golden harp above.

HYMN

H Y M N LXXXV.

WHEN Jesus darts his glorious light,
  All heaven is ravish'd with the sight,
The Cherubs strike their golden lyres,
The Seraphs glow with brighter fires:
  But when Jesus shews his face,
  All are hushed and lost in praise!

H Y M N LXXXVI.

1 IN vain are children taught to pray,
  Or praise a God unknown
Christ is the true and living Way,
  And God and Christ are one.

2 Whene'er we think on God Most High,
  Whene'er his praise proclaim,
We think on Him, who stooped to die,
  We bow to Jesu's name.

3 My God in Jesus reconciled,
  Declare thyself to me,
If still an uncorrupted child,
  Yet still I know not Thee.

4 To make my sinful nature pure,
  Thy Spirit, Lord, impart,
And me from actual sin secure,
  By dwelling in my heart.

H Y M N LXXXVII.

O Might I in my youthful days
  Reflect on my Creator's grace,
Call on my heavenly Father's name,
Whose mercy made me what I am,
Whose love out of his bosom gave
His only Son, a world to save,
To buy, and wash me with his blood,
And bring my new-born soul to God.

HYMN

H Y M N LXXXVIII.

1 CHILDREN have a right to fing
Praifes to their Infant-King,
Tell how Chrift the holy Child
God and man hath reconciled.

2 Whom the heavens cannot contain,
Very God and very man,
God was in his infancy
Weak and ignorant like me.

3 Wherefore did he ftoop fo low ?
Jefus, help my heart to know,
Thou who didft my flefh receive,
Unto me thy Spirit give.

4 Thus explain the myftery;
Then I fhall be one with Thee,
Then I fhall above the fky
Endlefs hallelujahs cry.

H Y M N LXXXIX.

1 TO God the Creator of all
My earlieft tribute I pay,
On Him with humility call,
And promife his laws to obey :
I promife alas, but in vain,
Unlefs He his Spirit beftow,
From folly and fin to reftrain,
And keep me wherever I go.

2 O Father of mercies, attend,
(Though now I in ignorance cry,)
And teach me on Him to depend,
My Advocate there in the fky.
Whatever I afk in the name
Of Jefus, I hear, fhall be done,
As due to that innocent Lamb,
As claiméd by thine heavénly Son.

HYMN

H Y M N XC.

1 LET all that breathe, Jehovah praise,
  Almighty, all-creating Lord,
Let earth and heavén his powér confefs,
  Brought out of nothing by his word!
He fpake the word, and it was done,
  The univerfe his word obeyéd:
His Word is his eternal Son,
  And Chrift the whole creation made.

2 Jefus the Lord and God moft high,
  Maker of all mankind and me,
Me Thou haft forméd to glorify,
  To know, and love, and live for Thee:
Wherefore to Thee my heart I give.
  (But Thou muft firft beftow the powér)
And if on earth for Thee I live,
  Thee I fhall foon in heavén adore.

H Y M N XCI.

1 WHO fhall join the acclamation
  Of that bright celeftial quire,
While with raptérous exultation
  All in fongs of praife afpire?
  Hallelujah
Sounds from evéry tuneful lyre.

2 I, if here I love my Lover,
  Here my heart to Jefus give,
When this mortal life is over,
  Shall an harp and crown receive,
  Hallelujah
Sing, as long as God fhall live.

H Y M N XCII.

1 THE Judge of all fhall foon come down
  Bright on his everlafting throne
Summon the nations to his bar,
And I fhall take my trial there.

2 Jefus,

3 Jefus, be now my Friend with God,
And wafh me in thy precious blood,
That at thy laft appearance I
May fhouting meet Thee in the fky.

HYMN XCIII.

1 HAPPY beyond defcription he,
Who in the paths of piety
Loves from his birth to run :
Its ways are ways of pleafantnefs,
And all its paths are joy and peace,
And heavén on earth begun.

2 If this felicity were mine,
I evéry other would refign
With juft and holy fcorn;
Cheerful and blith my way purfue,
And with the promiféd land in view,
Singing to God return.

HYMN XCIV.

1 THOU, the great, eternal Lord,
Art high above our thought,
Wcrthy to be fearèd, adoréd
By thofe thy hands have wrought:
None can with thyfelf compare,
Thy glory fills both earth and fky :
We, and all thy creatures are
As nothing in thine eye.

2 Of thy great unbounded powér,
To Thee the praife we give,
Infinitely great, and more
Than heart can e'er conceive;
When Thou wilt to work proceed,
None thy purpofe can withftand,
Fruftrate the determinéd deed,
Or ftay thé Almighty hand.

3 Thou,

3   Thou, O God, art wife alone,
     Thy counfel doth excel,
  Wonderful thy works we own,
     Thy ways unfearchable ·
  Who can found the myftery,
Thy judgments deep abyfs explain?
  Thou whofe eyes in darknefs fee,
     And fearch the heart of man.

4   Thou the holy God and pure,
     Hateft iniquity,
  Evil Thou canft not endure,
     Or let it ftay with Thee:
  Who from fin refufe to turn,
Sinners with Thee fhall never dwell,
  But thy righteous wrath fhall burn
     After their fouls to hell.

5   Good Thou art, and good Thou doft,
     Thy mercies reach to all,
  Chiefly thofe on Thee who truft,
     And for thy mercies call:
  New they evéry morning are:
As Fathers, when their children cry,
  Us Thou doft in pity fpare,
     And all our wants fupply.

6   Mercy o'er thy works prefides,
     Thy Providence difplayéd
  Still preferves, and ftill provides
     For all thy hands have made;
  Keeps with more diftinguifhéd care
The man that on thy love depends,
  Watches evéry numberéd hair,
     And all his fteps attends.

7   Who can found the depths unknown
     Of thy redeeming grace,
  Grace which gave thy only Son
     To fave our ruinéd race!

Millions

Millions of tranfgreffors poor
Thou haft for Jefu's fake forgivén,
Made them of thy favour fure,
And fnatchéd from hell to heavén.

8 Millions more Thou ready art
To fave, and to forgive,
Evéry foul, and evéry heart
Of man thou wouldéft receive :
Father, now accept of mine
Which now through Chrift I offer Thee,
Tell a child, in love divine,
That thou haft pardonéd me.

H Y M N XCV.

1 O Father, I am but a child,
My body is made of the earth,
My nature alas, is defiléd,
And a finner I was from my birth ;
Not worthy to lift up my face
To a God on his heavénly throne,
Yet allow me to pray for thy grace,
For without it I muft be undone.

2 I cannot obey thy commands
Unaffifted by grace from above :
No grace I deferve at thy hands,
Yet I hope to recover thy love :
Thy mercy is promiféd to all,
The giver of Jefus Thou art,
And therefore attend to my call,
And difcover his love to my heart.

H Y M N XCVI.

1 TO me thy compaffion extend,
For the fake of thy heavénly Son,
From Satan and fin to defend,
And a world full of evil unknown :

An

An invisible enemy's power
   Ever near to destroy me I have,
A lion intent to devour ·
   Let mercy be nearer to save.

2 That mercy I languish to feel,
   If mercy infuse the desire,
My need of a Saviour reveal,
   My soul with the hunger inspire :
O Father, an infant allure
   In a way that I never have known,
And me by thy Spirit assure
   That mercy and Jesus are one.

HYMN XCVII.

1 COME, my companions dear,
   With mine your voices raise,
Let us with heart sincere
   Attempt our Saviour's praise,
And while our souls to heaven ascend,
Begin the song that ne'er shall end.

2   Of whom should children sing,
   But of that holy child
Who to their heavenly King
   Hath rebels reconciled ?
Peace upon earth he doth bestow :
Rejoice in God revealed below.

3   Who earth and heaven commands
   In years and wisdom grew,
Till seized by wicked hands,
   They wounded him and slew ·
But in his blood our peace is sealed,
And by his wounds our souls are healed!

4   Then let us bless his name,
   And thank him for his grace:
Worthy is Christ the Lamb
   Of universal praise.

Praise be on him by all bestowéd
Who lives, the one eternal God!

HYMN XCVIII.

1 MEET and right it is, that I
   Should my Maker glorify,
Born for this alone I am,
God to praise through Jesu's name:
Author of my life, receive
Praise the best a child can give.

2 Teach me as I older grow,
Thee in Christ aright to know,
That I may thy blessings prize,
Bring Thee Jesus sacrifice,
Thee with understanding praise,
Love, and serve Thee all my days.

HYMN XCIX.

1 PRAISE the Father for his love,
   Christ He sent us from above,
Publish the Redeemer's praise,
Bless the Spirit of his grace,
He reveals the Trinity,
Three in one, and one in three.

2 Glory be to God alone,
One in three, and three in one,
God from whom all blessings spring
Every child of *Adam* sing,
Praise him all ye heavénly host,
Father, Son, and Holy Ghost.

HYMN C.

1 THE Father above,
   The Son of his love,
We adore with the Spirit of grace,
Till he bids us arise,
To our throne in the skies,
And eternity spend in his praise.

FINIS.

Lightning Source UK Ltd.
Milton Keynes UK
UKOW041223070212

186816UK00007B/108/P